Isaiah's Gift of Hope
"Thy Will Be Done"

Written by
Crystal Cambisaca

"Joy Comes Through…"
Series

OSLP
GPS

One Smart Lady Productions
Gladstone Publishing Services

© 2015 Crystal Cambisaca

Independent Editing By: http://www. onesmartladyproductions.com
Publishing Imprint:
Gladstone Publishing Services: http://www. gladstonepublishing.com

ISBN 978-1-928681-16-8 – Paperback
ISBN 978-1-928681-17-5– eBook

Printed in the United States of America

Dedication

To our Sweet Isaiah, his one mission was to bring hope to

the hopeless.

"The Spirit of the Sovereign LORD is on me, because the LORD has anointed me to proclaim good news to the poor. He has sent me to bind up the brokenhearted, to proclaim freedom for the captives and release from darkness for the prisoners." NIV. Isaiah 61:1

Foreword

Gladstone Publishing Services dedicates the "Joy Comes Through..." book series to all who have lost loved ones young and old through death, divorce or separation. It is our desire each story is a blessing to help you through your own personal experience.

"Joy" is one of the nine gifts we receive from the Holy Spirit when we commit our life to Christ. The gifts are already with us even during the dark, desperate times in our lives. It is the second gift given after "Love ". We only have to draw from our faith and hope in God's promise. If "we seek God and his righteousness, all things shall be given to us"; even the mending of a broken heart.

Deborah Wilson Smart
Author of "Joy Comes Through the Mourning"

Introduction

My name is Crystal Cambisaca. I would like to share my story about my son Isaiah and how through his death brought us life.

It was April 2002, I was 16 years and Eladio, my boyfriend, was just 17. He was the type of boy who was very charismatic and one who had many girls. When he asked me to be his girlfriend just two days after meeting, I couldn't be happier. So I thought. It wasn't long before I knew his ways and would hear about him with other girls. Still for some reason I still wanted him to be mine.

There was a time that we broke up for about a year. I remember thinking about him a lot even praying that God would bring us together and make us close. Little did I know why I was praying so hard. I knew about Jesus growing up. We were even involved at church when I was younger but once I got into my teenage years (when you need God the most) my father started working on Sundays and church became less important.

During these years, I had experienced with alcohol and marijuana. That became my daily routine to smoke marijuana and get high and party. Soon after hanging out again in the fall of 2003 we were back together. I thought it was too good to be true since this time around Eladio was the one who was crazy about me. It was not long before I discovered I was pregnant. You never think it could happen to you until it does. At first, we were both happy but very nervous. We were just 18 and 19 did not know what to expect.

Knowing how Eladio was in the past, my parents were not happy but eventually they got used to the idea. A few months past and before I knew it Eladio was back to his old ways. I remember being depressed and crying a lot over him just really confused and didn't know what was going to happen in our future. He was around sometimes and sometimes not. Thank God that I had a great support team at home with my family.

Chapter One

When the time came for my first ultrasound, we were very excited. The technician performing the ultrasound had suddenly left the room and returned with the doctor to check out the ultrasound. He told us that our baby had what's known as *gastroschisis*. It is a rare birth defect, which they have seen more and more with no explanation.

Gastroschisis is when the intestines of the baby are outside of the body. It is when the stomach never closes with the intestines inside. They told me it was treatable but, of course, every case is different and could not say for sure how long the baby would stay at the hospital.

I could not believe what I was actually hearing. Is this even real? I was devastated. Eladio then drove me home and took off like normal. Later, I found him driving around with his friends like nothing ever happened. We just found out our child was sick and it was like nothing to him. I remember falling to my knees and crying out for the Lord to heal my baby.

Now I was considered high risk. I had frequent doctor appointments and ultrasounds. When I went to find out that, it was a boy Eladio was not there. I was happy but sad because Eladio was not there to share the joy.

My doctor's office was around the block from where Eladio's friend had lived. After leaving my appointment, we drove by to find Eladio and his friends hanging out having fun. Here, I was left with the responsibilities of being a pregnant teen.

When Eladio found out that, the baby was a boy, he wanted to name him after him. However, I loved the name Isaiah. Although he didn't agree with me on the name, we finally decided on Isaiah Eladio.

Preparing for Isaiah, I was so blessed with gifts. My father had painted and prepared a beautiful nursery. During one of my weekly ultrasounds, my doctor suggested inducing me a few weeks early because the baby's intestines were starting to knot off and block his blood flow.

I wasn't even sure if Eladio would even make it to his birth or not. The day before my induction, they brought me in for an amniocentesis, which is a very long thin needle they stick into your amniotic fluid to see if the baby's lungs are developed enough.

Once performing this, they discovered that his fluid was dark, which indicated the baby was under stress. They told me they had to take the baby that day. They said I had the option to be induced, but if the baby's heart rate drops or anything, we will need an emergency cesarean.

I don't like the word emergency anything so I opted to just have a normal cesarean that wasn't an emergency. We called Eladio and his family and they came. Although I was scared to death, I was happy he was there with me.

I remember hearing Isaiah's first cry which there are no words to describe…it was just beautiful! I never got to see him though. They took him right away to surgery. They even took Eladio and my mom to sign consent forms.

In the recovery room, everyone came in to see me. I

especially remember my sister because we both have fair skin and turn so red when we cry. She was a dark red that day. I asked her what was wrong, but she didn't say. Then Eladio came in with pictures of my baby who didn't look anything like I expected. He was beautiful but not dark like his Daddy.

Eladio is from Ecuador with dark features and I always imagined my children to be as dark as he was. That was not the case, well at least, not at first.

I remember returning to my room and everyone was depressed. While I waited, no one told me the truth about my baby. The head surgeon finally came and said that if the baby made it through the night it would be a miracle.

Since later in my pregnancy his intestines had knotted off it cut off the blood supply. By the time they took him, 90% of his small intestines were no good. Now left with just 10%, he was too little to be able to digest any food. He would now be fed fluids through an IV.

I remember Eladio taking me into see the baby. There he was just 5lbs 14oz hooked up to all these tubes and wires everywhere. Not the way any mother wants to look at her child. I could not hold him or even touch him much, but I loved him instantly.

When the time came for me to go home and leave him there, it was horrible. After about 5 days, we were able to hold him. He no longer had his breathing machine but other wires and tubes. I wanted to take him home so bad.

They told me that we could visit as much as we wanted. He was not able to have any milk even though I was pumping like crazy to give him the best. He sure loved his pacifier though. Eventually, when he could have milk at the most he ever had was just 3 teaspoons, which was gone in a second.

He would then have diarrhea or vomit immediately. Which then they would stop feeding for a while and increase his IV fluids. This always set us back.

Eladio stayed by my side the whole time and becoming a great father. Eventually, we were able to bring his own clothes and things from home which was nice. We were very hands on with his care and all his needs. They would allow us to bathe him even change and clean around his tubing. He had a scar on his belly around his drain where he should have had a belly button. I always said that we shared that in common that we were both left with our scars.

Isaiah had a total of four (4) abdominal surgeries, which for everyone was so hard. To sign his consent forms was tough, and then to say goodbye as they took him off to surgery; we would cry every time. Then waiting around and seeing him miserable and in pain was so bad. It hurt my heart. There were no words for how beautiful it was to hear him for the first time. Now there were no words to watch him in pain coming out of surgery and not being able to comfort him.

He had multiple procedures and a few spinal taps. Every day they took his blood, poked, and prodded him but still, he remained to be such a happy little baby. He was always, cooing and trying to talk with us…and everyone around him for that matter.

Eventually, once he was 3 months old, they had moved him from the NICU (Natal Intensive Care Unit) to a private room on another floor. At first, I thought this was not good but it turned out to be a blessing for us. We had a private bathroom with a shower and we brought in an air mattress and made it our own little home. We did not have to visit anymore. We could now just stay and even sleep.

We tried to be as normal as we could but being in the hospital made that difficult. This was now the winter of 2004. Since we both had graduated high school the year before I was able to stay with him all day while Eladio went off to work. Eladio would leave in the morning and then return after his work shift in the evening.

The staff there was great. They also loved our child. I would stroll him around the hospital. I also had to stroll his IV bags too.

He loved to leave his room and to see people. I would stay there all day. I would leave to go home and get clothes or if I had to go to the store. I remember asking the staff to babysit for me when I would step out. They would always laugh.

Sometimes I would return and one of the volunteer grandmothers would be rocking him or giving him attention, which he loved. Family and friends would also come and visit us. I remember Eladio's mother would stay on Friday nights so we could go home and my mother and aunt would come once a week and stay with him for a few hours so we could have a break.

I look back and see how blessed we were to have spent the time we did with our son. Not every child there had a family that is able or even willing to come and stay with them, which is very sad. We witnessed that a lot. As the months passed, I watched Eladio completely change and become this awesome father who truly loved his son.

Isaiah had a great Christmas. He even had his own little light up Christmas tree that my aunt let us borrow. Presents filled all around it too. I remember Christmas morning; he was so happy and smiling so much.

Chapter Two

When Isaiah was five months old, his doctor told us that out of a one-in-ten, his liver function was a high nine, which was dangerous. They said he would need a transplant right away. The IV fluids ended up ruining his liver. We had no idea what was going to happen next.

They told us that we had one day to prepare. They told us a private jet plane was going to bring Isaiah from Connecticut to Florida. We did not even know if we could even travel with him. Isaiah never even got to leave the hospital or even go outside this would be the first time for him.

They ended up letting us go with him, which was good. When our family came to say goodbye to us, they had no idea this would be the last time they would see Isaiah. Our pastor came and he prayed with us which was a great thing since we were both so afraid.

Our plane was so small only four other people were on

it besides us. It was February 2, 2005, and so cold outside in Connecticut and 70 degrees in Miami.

Once we had arrived, Isaiah was cranky and very fussy, which was not like him at all. I thought because it got warm too quick, but the truth was his liver was not functioning properly; fluid was building up in his body and was putting pressure on his lungs making him very uncomfortable. Not even his favorite pacifier would comfort him.

I remember that the staff wasn't very friendly to us. My son loved watching television and when we got there, another little girl had the only television they had in that room.

When I asked the nurse to please let my son watch it when she was finished, her response was sarcastic. "A five-month-old who watches TV?"

I said, "Yes he loves TV. He has been a hospital baby and that's what he does in his crib."

We did have one nurse there that was very sweet and kind to us. Seeing all the kids there post-transplant in pain and crying was scary.

We were able to stay at the Ronald McDonald's house,

which was nice and great because we did not have to pay anything. I remember the next morning praying with women from my church. We prayed that God would bring us with other Christian families.

Later that day getting off the elevator going to see the baby, we heard some people praying in Spanish so fervently or with so much authority that it freaked me out.

I remember staying a while with him and he was more and more uncomfortable he only wanted to be propped up on his boppy pillow. I remember his oxygen sensors were a little low they told me they would tap him which was a procedure they used to take some fluid out.

I can still remember so clearly saying goodbye to him as he was asleep and giving him a kiss. When I was closing up the rail of his crib, I looked down and seen him looking back up at me with his binky as if to say he loved me too. I have such a sweet memory of my baby. Not knowing that would be the last time, I would see him awake.

Chapter Three

That night we went to bed and got a call from the hospital telling me that my son stopped breathing and to get there as quick as we could. Even though we were just two blocks away, it seemed like forever.

When arriving it was such a scary sight to see them working on my little baby to get him to breath. They had put him on a machine called an oscillator. The oscillator was so strong they had to sedate him.

Soon after they were able to stabilize Isaiah, his doctors came to speak to us. They told us even if his organs come in that he could not have the surgery. Being on the oscillator, he would not make it. I felt that they were all so negative there.

My baby had already endured so much in just five short months surely this would all pass too. After hearing such bad news, I knew I had to go and call my parents and have everyone start praying. Eladio told me he was not going to leave his son's side. So I went by myself and called and spoke to my Dad.

Then I went to the sanctuary they had in the hospital and I went in and instead of praying on my knees I was so desperate, I fell completely on my face and cried out to the Lord. I prayed that even if my son were to be sick not to take him because I would be the best mom that I could be. I never prayed so hard in my life.

I went upstairs and couldn't find Eladio anywhere? He soon came to me with a smile on his face and with so much peace. I did not understand because I just left him crying. He then brought me to three Hispanic couples that were there because one of their young daughters had pneumonia.

They found him crying over my son and invited him to come and talk with them. Could this be the same people I heard praying earlier the day before? They were so kind to us.

They would drive one hour to pick us up and bring us to church; to eat and even would bring us to their house. These people were so filled with God's love that you wanted what they had. They demonstrated God's love to us. If you were not a Christian just by being around them, you would want to be.

Another couple who was always at the hospital with their daughter would always share God's word with us even giving us a Bible. Everyone was great especially knowing that we didn't have anyone else there. Could this be the answered prayer that me and the woman from my church prayed for?

I remember going with them one evening to church and wow, they worshiped for four hours. Our first Sunday I had to wear a translator since this was a Spanish service. I remember the pastor calling anyone to the front with a medical problem and I knew I had to go. So I took my translator off and walked up. It was not long before Eladio was right beside me. As they began praying over us, we both fell right to the ground and had indescribable peace. I've seen this before but never understood until I experienced it for myself.

I remember the following week. There was this woman who spoke to us about her oldest daughter. She died years before with heart problems. She also shared that God gave them Hope, the daughter she had after the death of her oldest.

It was a great testimony of what they went through, but I never thought for once that Isaiah was going to die. I felt God was just going to heal him and that would be it.

We continued going with them to church and wanted to even get married while we were there. We knew that was what God would want for us to do; to bless our family.

Due to immigration laws in Miami we were not able to. Eladio came from Ecuador when he was 14 years old and he was illegally in this country. This made it impossible for us to marry there. We had prayed with the pastor there promising to marry as soon as we could and to live under God as if we were.

Chapter Four

Going back and forth to the hospital every day I would see children who already had transplants and were back with complications. One day we were in the elevator with a mother of one of these children and she told me that a transplant was not a cure just another set of problems.

I did not really know much. I thought once he had his transplant that he would be better off than his current condition. Now the doctors told us before that he would be on medications for the rest of his life and would not have a normal life after transplant. I did not care I was willing to take it as long as my boy was with me here on this earth.

I would speak to my family every day back home who were once again attending church and they would tell me that my aunts, uncles, and cousins everyone was going. I did not realize the impact my son's sickness had on people getting their lives back to God. That was an awesome experience to see how the Lord was already using my son to bring us all back where we needed to be; back with the Lord where we belonged.

We were there a few weeks now and my parents would keep asking if they wanted us to come down and I would always say we were fine. Our families would send us money to eat and to get things we needed.

We started to know more and more families especially from the Ronald McDonald's house that we would constantly share our faith. We had made many friends there. The doctors would come and always seem to bring us bad news about our son. Always negative and that was the last thing we needed.

They would tell us that we would soon reach a limit. One young doctor even told me that if it were his child he would have said goodbye a long time ago. I asked if he had a child and he said no. I told him that if Jesus were to come for Isaiah that these machines would not keep him alive and if he did not come for him, then I would never unplug him. I never wanted to feel like we unplugged him.

It got to the point whenever the doctors would do their rounds I just wouldn't listen because it was never good. It was like the devil would speak through them always trying to bring us down. The closer we became with the Lord, the worse it seemed.

I remember speaking out loud telling the devil that he wasn't going to win. That even if my son were to die, he would live. That God would be the one taking him. We would still serve the Lord no matter what the outcome.

They tried a few times to wean him off this powerful breathing machine unto a lesser machine, but he never could handle it. I was there every time they had tried. I was there praying, but it never worked. I knew as long as he was on this machine he never had a chance of getting his transplant.

One night Eladio stepped out, and I was in our room just cleaning up and I prayed. I prayed, "Lord Isaiah was your baby way before he was ever mine. I know you love him even more than I and if it is your will to take him then, please give us peace we need to let go. Above all, it's **NOT MY WILL BUT YOURS!**"

Later that night we went to visit our son and that is when the doctors told us they had reached the limit and he probably would not last through the night. At this point, my precious Isaiah had about twenty different machines connected to his body, tubes and wires everywhere. All his other organs were starting to shut down he even began to develop fluid in the brain and internal bleeding.

This was not good. This could not really be happening. Looking down at my beautiful baby that brought us so much joy, my heart just broke looking at my son there just waiting.

Waiting on the Lord. (Isaiah 40:31 *Those that wait upon the Lord Shall renew their strength; They shall mount up with wings like eagles, They shall run and not be weary, they shall walk and not faint.*) Can you imagine holding your child's hand as you wait for the Lord to come and take him home?

It finally came time to say goodbye to our little boy. I said, "Isaiah mommy and daddy love you so much and we will miss you every day, but Jesus is coming to take you home, and baby you have to go."

I apologized if there was ever a time where I wasn't the

best mommy. I told him we would have brothers and sisters for him. We continued to hold his hands until finally the Lord came. My life, our life would never be the same.

I remember just watching them unplug every wire and every tube. It was really over I kept thinking. He was finally free my baby no longer would have to suffer.

After, I was able to hold him. I held him so tight and did not want to let go. I remember how peaceful and beautiful he looked. Finally, free.

Chapter Five

I kept thinking what I would give just to hold my baby again. I remember walking outside and looking up at the sky and life was just different. I just cannot explain it. It was like our burden that we carried with our son was gone. We did not have to worry anymore about it. The next challenge would be to live without him.

When we were sitting down outside, Eladio took my hand and told me that he would never leave me. We were in this together. It's a bond that only we share; because we shared the same loss.

I had to start making calls to everyone. I could not get a hold of my parents I knew they were on their way, which was a relief. The first person I contacted was my brother. I remember him saying, "Crystal I'm so sorry."

I told my brother life is too short for his grudge towards

the Lord and he told me he knew it. You see, five years earlier, my brother lost his wife from a heart attack. She left behind a 2 ½ yr old son and a 2-month-old daughter and my brother couldn't get over it. He even blamed God.

He even told me he wasted so many years hating God and said he was wrong. Shortly after, my parents had pulled up in a taxi. I was so happy to see them. They did not know anything yet, but my mother told me she had a feeling he was already gone.

I remember Eladio telling my father that it was the most horrible thing to watch your son suffer and there was nothing he could do about it.

At that moment, my father told Eladio, that he and our Heavenly Father shared something in common. While Jesus hung on the cross dying, the Father could do nothing if His will were going to be fulfilled. Just think, He was the God of the whole universe and he could not do anything.

I remember my mom just having such a hard time. It was I who did the one cooking for them. Everywhere we would go, people could not believe what we had just gone through, because of the peace we had.

Our friends there came shortly after to bring us their condolences. I honestly believe these people were a Godsend. He knew we needed theses special people to help prepare us for what was about to come. Isaiah's body was being flown back to Connecticut and our family and friends were coming in for his funeral, and we needed to get back home.

We checked different flights and they were too expensive for all of us to fly home. The cheapest was about $1,600. Where were we going to get that? Later one night a call came to our room with a lady on the other end telling us we leave in 2 days completely free of charge even our taxi to bring us to the airport was already tipped.

Wow, we have no idea to this day who paid our tickets, but I do know that this miracle was from the Lord. Through this whole experience, God always provided. Later before leaving, our friends had brought us a cd by "Third Day", a contemporary Christian group. I had picked a song called "My Offering" to play for his funeral.

You see the numbers 3 and 7 were very unique to us.

Three (3) is the Trinity-Father, Son and Holy Spirit. Jesus rose on the 3rd day. Isaiah was born on the 3rd day of the month, went to Florida on the 3rd day, died on the 3rd day and we ended up burying him on the 3rd day.

The creation story covers 7 days. God created the world in six and rested on the 7th day. Seven (7) means completion or perfection. Isaiah was my parent's 7th grandchild and he also was in bed space 7 in the ICU in Florida. We would always see those numbers 3 and 7 wherever we were. The plane that was paid in full was Flight 370. Since then, these numbers always grab our attention.

It was time for us to head back home and I was it was very sad because I always pictured bringing Isaiah home with us. We never did get that opportunity. I remember walking through the front door of my house and everyone was there.

My niece was right there waiting for me said, "You told me you were going to bring the baby home with you."

She would always ask me on the phone when he would be coming home and I would tell her soon. She only was able to see Isaiah once or twice here at our local hospital due to rules they had about children visiting. Although she lost her mother when she was a few months old, she had no idea of what death really was.

Seeing his room with all his things was heartbreaking. All my family was very supportive and very helpful putting everything together. This was great since my mind could not make any decisions at this point. I was pretty numb with so many emotions.

Every day was something different like being on a roller coaster. Some days were better than others were. Some days I felt like I just could not breathe or go on. These days I had to rely on God's strength because I had none. (Philippians 4:13 *I can do all things through Christ, who strengthens me.*)

Chapter Six

One of our pastor's from our local church came to our house to prepare the funeral. I remember him asking me why I chose Isaiah's name. I said that it was beautiful to me and he told me that Isaiah in the Bible came to lead a nation back to God. That is exactly what my son was on this earth for to lead us back to the God that we left. He came to let us know about God's salvation. Isaiah's name means salvation is of the Lord. (Isaiah 6:8 *Also I heard the voice of the Lord, saying: 'whom shall I send and who will go for Us?' Then I said, 'Here am I! Send me.'*) Later that evening I remember going to the funeral home and everyone was able to view his little body, but I just could not bear it. Thank God I never looked because I wouldn't want that to be my last vision of him.

The last time I saw my son he was beautifully free. The next day seemed like the worst day when we had to go lay his body to rest. Although he wasn't there, he was with Jesus, it was so hard letting go of the body that I used to hold and kiss. I remember I dreaded the whole day and was in a completely foggy state; like being on drugs minus the drugs.

It was so hard. I cannot remember all who came although I remember many people. One very clear memory I do have is sitting in the front row and my Uncle behind me tapping me on the shoulder telling me that he got saved because of my baby. Imagine that God using my child to advance his kingdom.

I remember looking back as we drove to the cemetery and there were so many cars following. I felt honored to have all these people come support us during this difficult time.

I do remember, some of the first people to show up were his nurses. His very first nurse, when he was born was there. You have to know these people loved Isaiah too after all he was their baby also. It was so cold that day and all I remember just holding on to Eladio as tight as I could.

We made a thing out of going to clean his stone and bring flowers every week after church. It was comforting and helped in our grieving. I remember days, weeks, months and even the years following were very hard. I still miss him and always will. I still cry for him and cry out for the Lord's comfort. I remember about a week after his funeral I was laying in bed one morning because I didn't sleep much thinking that I really needed to write a book later that morning.

I go downstairs to where my parents were and my father asked me if I ever thought of writing a book to tell this story. Was this confirmation or what? It took years but here it finally is. A few months later the same Uncle who said because of my son, he asked Jesus to save him was bringing friends to church who had a teenage son who had leukemia.

As that boy would go to church, he gave his life to the Lord and was saved. A few weeks later he died. Although this was heartbreaking, I had an inner joy that this whole thing with him going to church and finding Jesus all started with a little baby sick in the hospital.

I had a talk with my father that this was the joy that came with our testimony through our son's death. That because our son's death brought life to others brought joy to my heart.

Talking with my father about Isaiah always brought tears to his eyes. You have to understand that my father was saved back in the 70s but through the years his fire burnt low. Once Isaiah came and especially after he left, my father's flame turned into a full blown bonfire.

So many lives were impacted through my son. I remember one day just having a terrible day in my room crying out to the Lord why me? Why us?

I remember not hearing an audible voice, but I felt it so strong in my spirit. God told me, *"It's not that I am punishing you for the bad things you have done, but I am blessing you because of all the good things."*

It hit me then I wasn't being punished but blessed. Having him for the time we had was a blessing. To know him to hold him to love on him was all a blessing from the Lord that I would not trade. Although I miss him like crazy, I feel so privileged that God chose to use us to bring this special child into the world.

Chapter 7

A few months later Eladio and I were married. Our pastor told us that couples who were married for years could not go through what we did. He said we were special because we endured many things together before ever being married.

We knew this is what was missing in our life that we wanted God to bless us in our unity. Although we were very young getting married and going through all this, we have also been so blessed in our life. It is like we were in an elevator that was moving up much quicker than others around us.

That was also a prophecy that was spoken over us, and I have seen it manifested through the years. I know that not everyone knows exactly why things happen in their lives or why tragedy exists. I know for us it was to bring us to a place in God that we needed to be. God allowed our son to get our attention focused back on him because when there is nothing left you will cry out to the Lord.

I always catch people off guard when I tell them that my first child passed. Immediately they say, "I'm so sorry."

I always respond with, "Don't be sorry because this is my blessing."

We have since moved to North Carolina where God has planted us in a local church with some pretty awesome people. We hope to be used by God to help bring comfort to those who have been through the death of a child.

Through our testimony, we bring them hope. (2 Corinthians 1:3 *Blessed be the God and Father of our Lord Jesus Christ, the Father of mercies and God of all comfort. Who comforts us in all our tribulation, that we may be able to comfort those who are in any trouble, with the comfort with which we ourselves are comforted by God.*)

As I finally write this book, it has been 8 years since the passing of Isaiah. I think of him daily. I wish he could have stayed around, but I know that everyone has a purpose and a plan. When your purpose is fulfilled, it is time to go home. I'm so happy as I prayed that even if my son was sick to leave him here with me that God did not grant that prayer that he allowed his perfect will to be done.

I believe we pray all the time for our will and what we want, but I am sure happy that I finally prayed for God's perfect will. The hope that the Lord has given me is that Isaiah is not dead but alive and well. One day when my purpose is fulfilled, I will go where he is and I will be with him for all eternity.

We now have a healthy two-year-old little boy named Eladio Jeremiah, who is completely healthy and who brings us so much joy. He does not replace Isaiah in any way, but God has used him to restore our family. I know the Lord has great plans in store for our family. We appreciate our son even more so because we know how losing a child is.

We waited 7 years for our second child and we couldn't be happier.(Matthew 5:4 *Blessed are they that mourn for they shall be comforted.*)

God is so good to us. We are not perfect, but God's not done with us yet. I pray this book will help many who are or who have gone through any loss. To know, there is a God, who has a perfect will for your life.

When I find myself crying for Isaiah I just cry to the Lord and tell him if all my pain and suffering is to bring Him glory then, this whole thing was well worth it.

If I do not use my pain and my joy to bring it back to Him, then Isaiah coming and going was really for nothing at all. He sees the greater picture. Just to think this, all started because a young 16-year-old girl prayed for the boy she loved.

Epilogue

Message from Crystal Cambisaca

Isaiah passed on February 23, 2005 and we were married that July. We moved a year later to North Carolina where we bought our first home a few short months later. It has now been eight years, and we have a three-year-old handsome little boy named Eladio, and a precious 10-month-old daughter named, Solaiah. We have been serving in our local church's Hispanic service since 2009, where I am the site director for our children's ministry.

We welcomed our third gift Solaiah on November 23, 2013. She was a huge ten pound, five ounces, twenty-three inches long beautiful baby girl. We chose this name because Sol means "sun" in Spanish and she is definitely a ray of sunshine for us. The ending of her name "aiah" is from Isaiah. Solaiah being so big was a surprise although; I felt every ounce of her towards the end of my very uncomfortable pregnancy. She was born and had low blood sugar so once again we were faced with another child in the ICU. This was heartbreaking because I've always prayed for healthy children and now I had to leave yet another baby in the ICU as I was discharged.

It was very trying. I asked God why this? Why now? It brought us back to the place with Isaiah and it wasn't a good feeling. I had to really just rely on God. I kept reminding Him of all the years I prayed for healthy children. I'm not quite sure why this had to happen. After five days on Thanksgiving, we were able to bring her home. Shortly after I ended up with a very bad infection from my cesarean and needed medical care for the next month. It was very hard, but God is always faithful and provided us with a lot of great family and friends to help. As I write this, Solaiah is almost a year old and such a precious little girl. I always thought little Eladio resembled Isaiah until Solaiah came along. She looks just like Isaiah, which is so sweet and just a little reminder of how good God truly is.

Little Eladio is now three and so full of life plus a whole

lot of energy. He is super smart and such a blessing. We talk to him all the time about Isaiah and he knows he is in heaven. He often talks about going to heaven so he can play with him. One day as we were in the car Eladio asked me to tell him the story about Isaiah. I always say that my baby was very sick and then Jesus took him to heaven. I tell Eladio, Mommy was very sad but then Jesus gave Mommy another baby and he yells, "That's me That's me." I say, "Yes Eladio that was you." And he says, "Yes mommy I fixed your broken heart."

Isaiah's tenth birthday just passed and he asked me if his brother was going to have a piñata. I told him he was going to have the best piñata there is in heaven. Later that day little Eladio came to me and said, "Mommy, we forgot to go to Isaiah's birthday party in heaven." It's amazing how only at three his mind works. He sees heaven as a place not far away, just take a plane to the clouds.

I think we all should view heaven this way. I told him we couldn't go to heaven just yet because if we could go to visit we wouldn't want to leave. I think about my life and all I went through since Isaiah and although sometimes it seems unbearable I'm thankful for the relationship I have developed with the Lord and just how much he loves me. I once heard this and it makes so much sense, God only calls a few people into such a close relationship with him as those parents who lose children and have to totally rely on him. That to me is how I sum this all up. I'm not sure what God has for us in the future, but I'm pretty sure he will use us in a mighty way to help other parents who like us lost a child. Our testimony will indeed bring him Glory.

The Author

Crystal Cambisaca was born on June 4, 1985. She grew up in West Haven, CT. She attended and graduated from West Haven High School in 2003. Crystal met Eladio through mutual friends in 2002 right before her 17th birthday and gave birth to Isaiah on September 1, 2004 at 19 years old. Isaiah passed on February 23, 2005 and they were married that July.

Crystal and her family moved a year later to North Carolina where they bought their first home a few short months later. She wrote *Isaiah's Gift of Hope* and now 8 years after his death, was ready to publish. She and Eladio have two children; a handsome little boy named Eladio and their precious daughter named Solaiah.

Together they have been serving in their local church's Hispanic service since 2009. Crystal is the site Director for the children's ministry.

Psalms 30:2-5 (ESV)

2 O Lord my God, I cried to you for help, and
   you have healed me.

3 O Lord, you have brought up my soul from
   Sheol; you restored me to life from among
   those who go down to the pit.

4 Sing praises to the Lord, O you his saints, and
   give thanks to his holy name.

5 For his anger is but for a moment,
   and his favor is for a lifetime.
   Weeping may tarry for the night,
   but *joy comes with the morning*.

More From the

"Joy Comes Through" Series

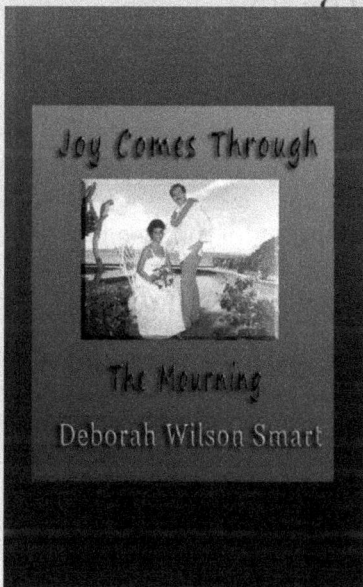

One Smart Lady Productions

Joy Comes Through

The Mourning

Deborah Wilson Smart

Widowhood Came Too Soon.
December 16, 2003

"In *Joy*, I share with you the tools which helped me transition through the grieving process. Letters, poems, prose and mind games I played to keep ward off depression."

D. W. Smart

http://smartbychoice.com

"The author paints a vivid and honest picture of her experience as a widow and compassionately invites the reader to join her on her pathway to peace."

Excerpt from the "Foreword" by Pastor George E. Holland, Sr. and First Lady Eartha Holland – Green Grove Baptist Missionary Church, West Berlin, New Jersey.

For more information go to Gladstone Publishing Services' Website
http://www.gladstonepublishing.com

The End

At 3:00 AM, December 16, 2003, my cell phone rang. I reached over and grabbed it from Donald's pillow. Why do these calls always come in the middle of the night?

"Hello?"

"Mrs. Karper? I'm so sorry, Mr. Karper passed away just a few minutes ago." The voice on the other end of the line said.

"Thank you. I'll be there," I said and hung up the phone. I laid there staring at the ceiling. I remember taking a deep breath and thinking, 'It's finally over. He's not in any more pain.'

I then dialed my girlfriend's number. She made me promise to call her, to not to go to the hospital or hospice without her. Unfortunately, I got her voice mail. I then tried to think of someone else close by to call. I really did not want to go alone. I remembered a woman at my office also said if I need anything at all to call. We had just become fast friends. We both were in children's publishing and had some things in common.

She answered the phone, and I explained what happened. She agreed to go with me. I picked her up and we took the fifteen-minute drive together. I told her that when I walked up the hill to the apartment, I looked up at the clear dark sky. The stars were everywhere, and I smiled and said, "Oh Donald, you picked a beautiful morning to go home."

We parked and rode the elevator up to the hospice floor. It was just one floor in a wing connected to Kennedy Hospital in Cherry Hill, New Jersey. We had just admitted Donald that evening about 8:00. Earlier the previous morning, I received a call from the Doctor on duty that Donald had a very bad night and was not doing well at all. I had expected him to tell me he was on his way back to the nursing home, so his bed would be again secure. Instead, he told me that it was just a matter of time. I was stunned. I remember asking him, "Are you referring to hospice?" He replied, "Yes."

That was it. The death sentence we hadn't heard during Donald's three-year battle with cancer. No one said that his sarcoma was fatal. He had two surgeries and participated in three clinical trials. Even though he was experiencing discomfort, he was always able to maintain his independence, and I was able to continue working. I thank God that I was self-employed, so I was able to control my hours.

When the elevator opened, it opened onto a floor with subdued lighting and decorated in pastels instead of the traditional hospital colors of green and putty. I walked to his room, and the nurse met me. Karen, my friend, asked if I wanted her to go in with her, I told her I would be all right. After all, it was Don.

I walked in and he looked so peaceful. I know that sounds like a cliché, but he had been in such pain over the past two weeks. They had placed his glasses on and smoothed out his covers. There was no rise and fall of his chest, just quiet. I sat down and placed my hand on top of his. I was surprised because his hand was still warm. Donald's hands had always been cold to the touch.

I spoke softly to him. I do not remember exactly what I said, but I am sure it had to do with him being out of pain. The nurse stepped in with a box of tissues. I turned, took the box and turned back to him. I had not cried yet, and I did not feel as if I would. We had been through so much, especially the last three weeks of his life. I think I was just relieved it was over.

Don knew how I felt about him; I knew how he felt about me that was all that mattered. There was nothing that I had to prove to anyone by crying. We shared a lot of time together just being in each other's presence. We also learned to pray together, and call on the Lord for strength to see us through. The Lord did. He blessed Don with a quick and peaceful death. I told everyone it was also a Christmas gift from Don. He said that Sunday, two days earlier, that he was dying. He knew it, and he was angry. He didn't want to leave me, and asked if I would stay with him until the end. Although I wasn't there when he took his last mortal breath, I was with him, and he is still very much a part of me.

You cannot live with a person, good or bad, for 21 years and not incorporate some of their essences into your being. *"Joy Comes through the Mourning"* is a celebration of my life as I live today in the Lord. They are prayers and thoughts I captured over the past year. It tells of my journey and challenges, and finally the triumph of my finding the true meaning of walking with the Lord.

www.ingramcontent.com/pod-product-compliance
Lightning Source LLC
Chambersburg PA
CBHW060539030426
42337CB00021B/4342